Originally published as *Willewete+. Het heelal* in Belgium and the Netherlands by Clavis Uitgeverij, 2019
English translation from the Dutch by Clavis Publishing Inc., New York

Visit us on the Web at www.clavis-publishing.com.

Want to Know+. The Universe written and illustrated by Daniëlle Futselaar

ISBN 978-1-60537-581-6

This book was printed in March 2020 at Graspo CZ, a.s., Pod Šternberkem 324, 76302 Zlín, Czech Republic.

First Edition
10 9 8 7 6 5 4 3 2 1

WANT TO KNOW

The
Universe

Daniëlle Futselaar

Clavis

NEW YORK

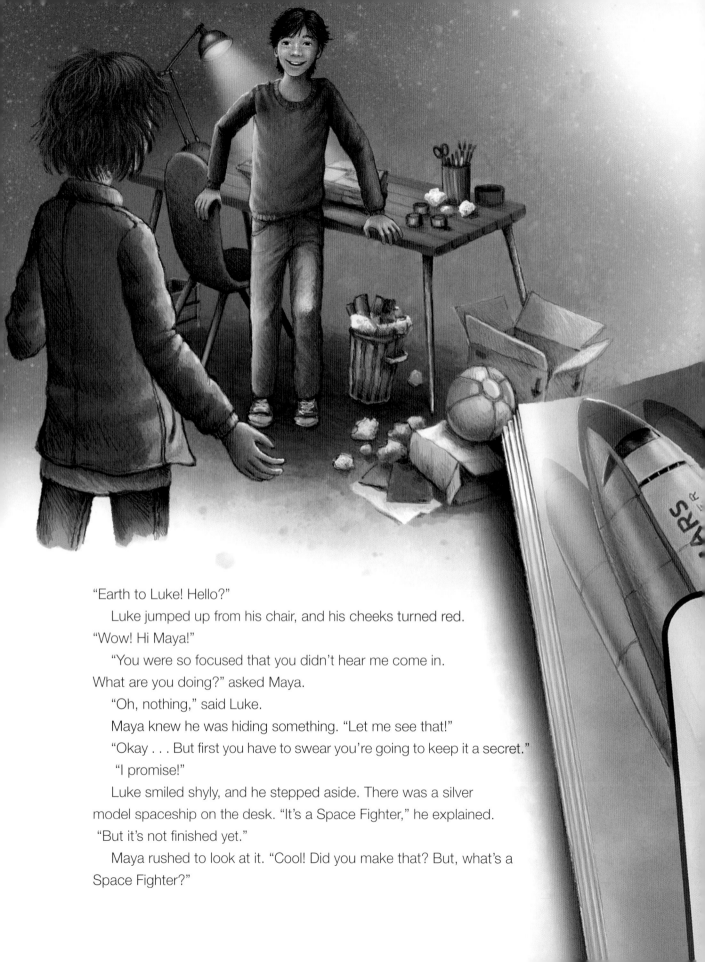

"Earth to Luke! Hello?"

Luke jumped up from his chair, and his cheeks turned red. "Wow! Hi Maya!"

"You were so focused that you didn't hear me come in. What are you doing?" asked Maya.

"Oh, nothing," said Luke.

Maya knew he was hiding something. "Let me see that!"

"Okay . . . But first you have to swear you're going to keep it a secret."

"I promise!"

Luke smiled shyly, and he stepped aside. There was a silver model spaceship on the desk. "It's a Space Fighter," he explained. "But it's not finished yet."

Maya rushed to look at it. "Cool! Did you make that? But, what's a Space Fighter?"

"And you call yourself a science fiction fan?" Luke laughed. "It's only the coolest space-ship in *Star Wars*! The Space Fighter is superfast and invincible."

"Nice. And you're making it just for fun?" Maya asked.

"No," Luke answered. With a grin that said he knew something she didn't, he took the latest issue of *The World of Science Fiction* from his desk and showed it to Maya.

WiN!

Have you always wanted to see a real spaceship? Enter our competition, and win a trip for two to **NASA in Florida!** Build or draw your ultimate spaceship, and send us a picture.

The creator of the most original and creative spaceship, and a guest, will witness the launch of a test flight of the Mars Cruiser.

The first steps

"*Pojechali!*" That's what Yuri Gagarin said on 12 April 1961, when he was launched into the cosmos with the spacecraft Vostok 1. The Russian astronaut became the first man in space. His cheer meant: "Here we go!"

The first man on the moon was the American astronaut Neil Armstrong. When he stepped onto the moon on 20 July 1969, he said the famous line: "That's one small step for men, one giant leap for mankind."

"I've been secretly working on it for days. If I win, you can come with me," said Luke.

"Really? To Florida?"

"Yes, but it's our secret, okay? We don't want anyone else to enter the competition, so I have a better chance of winning."

"Sure thing!" Maya promised. "I'll let you get back to work."

"Thanks," Luke responded. "I'll text you when it's finished. Okay?"

"Okay! May the Force be with you," Maya said solemnly.

Firework rocket

The first 'missiles' were made in China. They were shot into the air with gunpowder. Nowadays, gunpowder is still used in fireworks, but it's no longer used to launch real rockets.

Rocket daddy

In 1895, the Russian scientist Konstantin Tsiolkovsky invented a rocket that could fly on liquid fuel. With this invention, he laid the foundation for the modern space rocket. He is called "the father of spaceflight."

Luke sat down to really focus. He wanted to carefully paint all kinds of tiny details on the spaceship. It had to look as real as possible!

It was almost time for dinner when the detailed work was done. Luke looked up proudly from his project. It had turned out really well. The space rocket looked so realistic, with jet engines, windows, shutters, solar panels, and all kinds of buttons and lights. Luke wanted to run downstairs with the Space Fighter in his hands, but he knew that his family could never keep a secret. His sister was always on Snapchat, and his mother shared everything on Facebook. Every dull family moment, every picture of their dog or cat . . . even the hamster Yoda had to be shared and liked! He would keep things quiet at home for now. But he had promised to keep someone else informed.

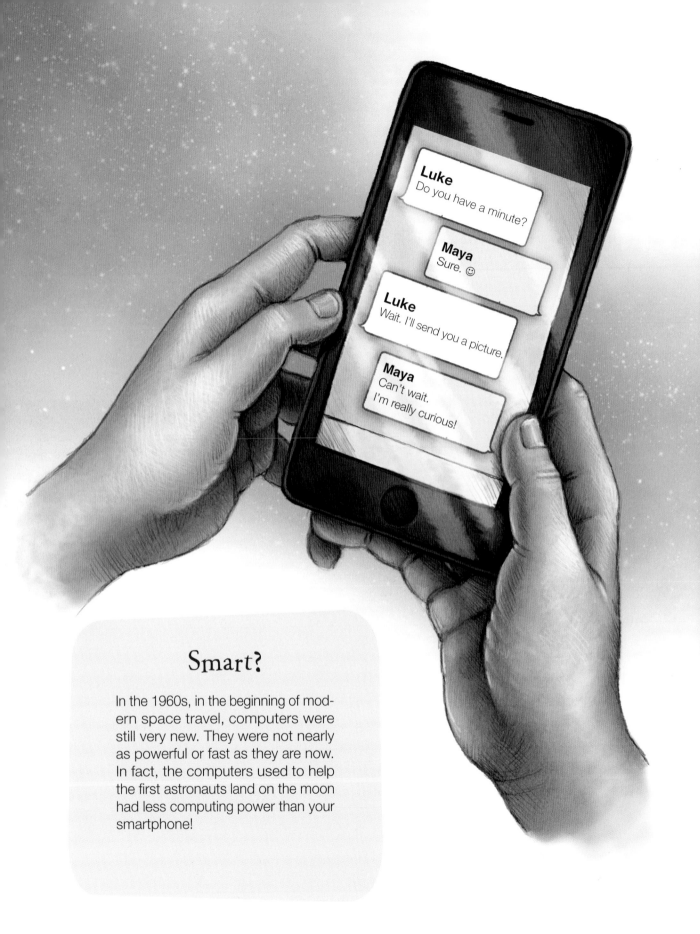

Smart?

In the 1960s, in the beginning of modern space travel, computers were still very new. They were not nearly as powerful or fast as they are now. In fact, the computers used to help the first astronauts land on the moon had less computing power than your smartphone!

A few days later, Luke was sitting on the couch, playing video games and snacking on corn chips. His dad sat down to join him when his phone rang.

"Hello."

"Yes, that's me . . ."

"Oh, really?"

"I'll tell him, thank you."

"Luke, that was a woman from *The World of Science Fiction* magazine. She mentioned a contest. Do you know anything about that?"

Luke dropped the controller. "Oh?" he asked carefully.

His father put his arm around Luke. "Well, she said your design came in second place. She said it was a really difficult choice. That's really good. I'm proud of you!"

From purpose to design

How do you design a spacecraft? That depends entirely on the purpose of the journey. For example, a rocket that brings people to the moon must have room for passengers. But that doesn't apply to a flight without a crew. And a spacecraft that wants to return to Earth also needs more fuel than a rocket that stays in space.

Luke couldn't hide his disappointment. He ran upstairs, fell on his bed, and pulled his pillow over his head. He wanted to disappear. He was so sure he was going to win, and now his chance to go to the launch was lost.

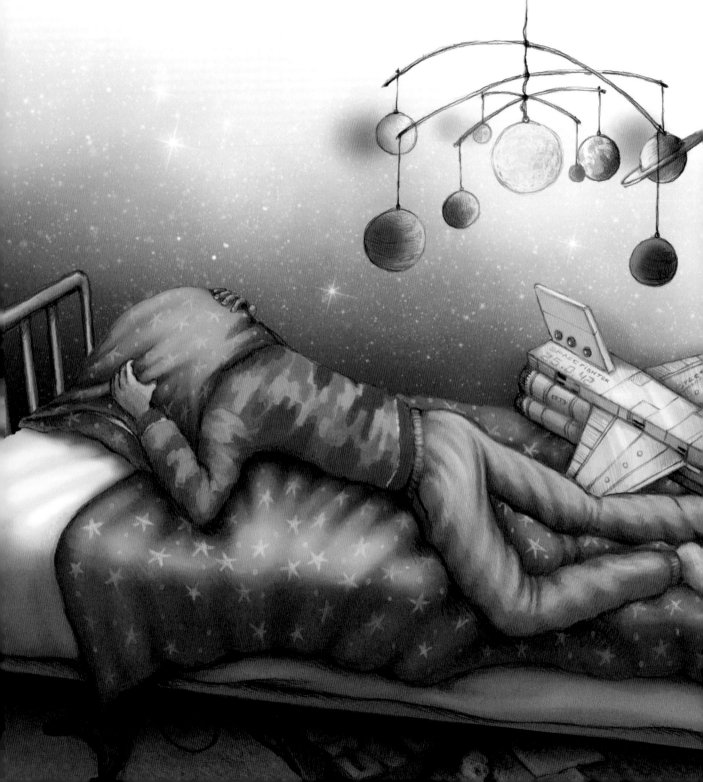

He imagined what it would have been like to be at the launch with Maya. He could picture them sitting in the VIP stand as the count down began. Three . . . Two . . . One . . . Lift-off! Luke could almost hear the roaring sound of the booster rockets and see the smoke and fire as the huge rocket started to take off on its way to Mars.

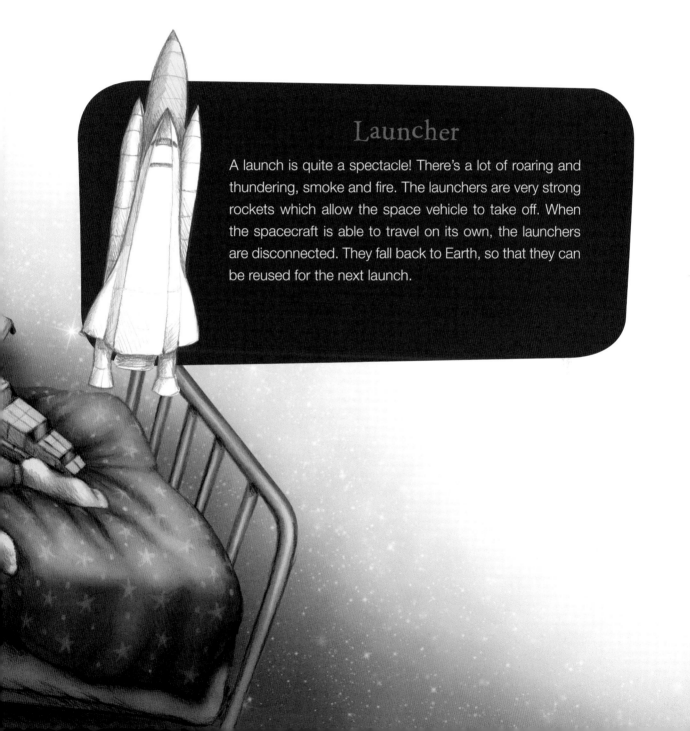

Launcher

A launch is quite a spectacle! There's a lot of roaring and thundering, smoke and fire. The launchers are very strong rockets which allow the space vehicle to take off. When the spacecraft is able to travel on its own, the launchers are disconnected. They fall back to Earth, so that they can be reused for the next launch.

Suddenly, there was a knock on the door.

"I just got another call," his father said. "From the magazine."

"Oh?"

"Yes, and the girl who came in first place isn't able to accept the prize."

Luke asked: "And?"

"And that means you won!"

"I won! I won!" Luke jumped out of bed and danced around the room with his arms in the air. He felt as if he was about to fly.

Luke
Guess what? ☺

Maya
What?

Luke
I won!
We are going to Florida!

Maya
Are you serious? I'm freaking out here!
☺

Weird space

According to some astronauts, space smells like seared steak, hot metals, and welding fumes.

Greetings from outer space

Twenty million dollars! That's how much American businessman Dennis Tito paid in 2001 to be the first tourist to go into space. In a Russian spacecraft, he flew to the International Space Station ISS, where he stayed for eight days.

Luke and Maya spent two days touring the NASA visitor centers and today it was finally the day for the launch.

"Look, there it is!" Luke pointed in the distance, to a big rocket in front of a tall hangar.

"Isn't this exciting?" said Maya.

"Oh yes," Luke answered. "But . . . I would really like to see it up close."

Maya's eyes started to sparkle. "Me too! But that's impossible, right?"

Luke and Maya looked around. The other visitors were focused on their binoculars and cameras. No one was watching them.

"Do you see those two buildings over there?" Luke said. "If we walk behind those, no one will notice us, and then we'll end up behind that tall hangar."

"If you do it, I'll do it too," said Maya.

Luke looked around again. He threw his backpack over his shoulder and grinned.

"Let's go! May the Force be with us!"

Holiday in space

Want to spend a week on Mars or go on a tour of the solar system? Unfortunately, that's not possible yet, but scientists are working toward the day when tourists can go to space.

They sneaked away from the other visitors to the tall hangar. But at the corner of the second building, Luke suddenly stopped. He dove behind a dumpster and pulled Maya with him.

"Hey, what are you doing?" Maya shrieked.

"Ssh," Luke hushed, pointing. "Look."

Two men approached. If Luke hadn't pulled his friend away, they would've been caught. From behind the dumpster, they peeked at the passing men.

One was wearing blue coveralls and a bright yellow safety helmet, the other was wearing a gray suit. It was clear that the two were arguing.

"Listen!" the man in the coveralls said. "We have to postpone! It's too dangerous!"

"No way," the man in the suit replied. "We've already lost millions. There've been too many mistakes in the communication. If we don't launch *today*, it will ruin us!"

The man in the coveralls kicked the dumpster and swore. Then he walked off grumbling.

"Gee, that was intense," Maya whispered.

"Did you hear what they were saying?" Luke asked.

"Yes, bizarre! Do you think there might be something wrong with the Mars Cruiser?"

"I don't know," Luke shrugged. "It's a test flight, so who knows."

Safety first

Launches are often postponed. Because the weather is bad, for example. But also when the team is not entirely sure that everything is working well. Every detail of the launch has to be right, because even a small mistake can have disastrous consequences. Space travel is very expensive, and in case of manned flights, human lives are at stake. Therefore, it's very important that everything runs smoothly.

They crept further toward the high hangar. When they saw a door there, they slipped inside. The hangar was empty, except for the enormous scaffolding and large metal stairs along the walls. Luke suspected that the Mars Cruiser had been built in this room.

Carefully, they climbed the stairs until they reached a big window. When they looked outside, the gigantic Mars Cruiser was right in front of them. It was getting prepped for the test flight. The launch would start any minute now. They had the best view, just like Luke had imagined!

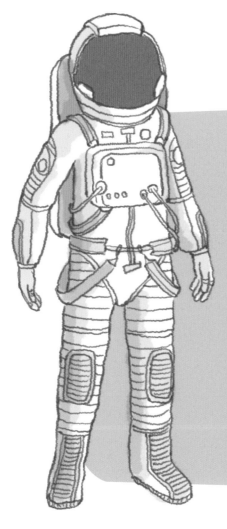

Safe in a spacesuit

Space is a dangerous place for people. You would freeze there, because it's about 454 degrees Fahrenheit below zero. And you might burn, because nothing is blocking the radiation from the sun. You would suffocate, because there's no oxygen. And your blood would start to bubble, because there's no atmospheric pressure . . . Luckily, a spacesuit would protect you from all that danger.

"Quiet!" Maya suddenly whispered. "I hear something."

The man in the coveralls came running up the stairs too. He seemed angry, because his loud footsteps echoed through the hangar.

"We have to get out," Luke said. "He can't see us in here."

Maya and Luke pressed their backs against the wall and looked around in panic. There was only one way out: a small corridor next to the window, that led to a small door and a room full of spacesuits. They ran off as quietly as possible.

Time for lift-off

When does the launch start? Astronauts start counting down very early, sometimes up to 96 hours in advance. There's still a lot to do: the spacecraft is put in the right place, fuel is delivered, all systems are checked, and so on. The moment of launching is called "T." If an astronaut says "T-minus ten seconds," it means that it is ten seconds before the launch.

But then Maya stopped running. "Hang on a minute . . ." she said. "I think we're in the cargo hold. We're *inside* the Mars Cruiser! This is wrong. We have to get out!"

But they were trapped, because the man in the coveralls was entering the cargo hold too. Luke and Maya hid behind the spacesuits.

Luke reached for Maya's hand, and they waited quietly, their hearts pounding with fear.

The man in the coveralls was talking to himself. "Why won't they listen to me? I've made this spacecraft with my own hands! No one knows more about it than I do!" He was pacing back and forth. "I know what to do."

He took a panel from the wall, pulled out a few electric wires, and put the panel back. The man looked around one more time and then walked away.

It took a while before Luke and Maya dared to breathe again. Only when they knew for sure that the man had left, they crawled out of their hiding place.

"Let's get out of here," Luke whispered. He sneaked up to the door, but the man had locked it behind him. Luke pulled the handle hard. It didn't budge. With all his strength, he tugged the handle, but he couldn't move it.

In the rocket, the screens suddenly blinked, and in the distance, a voice sounded through the speakers. "Countdown, T-minus ten seconds . . ."

"No!" said Maya. "They're counting down for the launch!" She pounded with two fists on the door. "Let us out! Please." But there was no one who could hear them.

Outside, the launch went exactly as Luke had imagined it would. The countdown, the smoke, the fire. Then everything started to shake and vibrate.

And the voice kept rattling: "Five . . . Four . . . Three . . . Two . . . One . . . We have lift-off."

"All systems active . . . Oxygen levels perfect."

The rocket took off, rattling and shaking. Luke and Maya were pushed hard to the ground and collapsed under the pressure. But after a while, it was as if Luke woke up from a wonderful dream. It felt as if he was floating in a swimming pool. Until he realized that he was really floating.

A few feet from him, Maya was also floating through space.

"Maya, wake up!" Luke screamed.

Maya opened her eyes with a fright and gasped for air. "We are in space! We're floating!" she yelled. "Wow!"

Luke tried to move toward Maya, but he had hardly any control over where he was going. "This whole being weightless thing isn't easy," he said.

"Wait," said Maya, laughing. She swam toward a wall, pushed off, and floated to Luke with a forward roll.

Luke imitated her, and in no time at all they did somersaults and cartwheels through the hold of the rocket. "Whee!"

Floaty

Gravity is the natural force that causes things to fall toward the earth. When you jump in the air, the earth pulls you back to the ground. But when you go into space, that force becomes less strong: the further away from a planet, the less force of attraction there is. That's why you can float in space.

Fast growing

Since there's much less gravity in space, everything floats around. People, objects . . . even splashes of cola! And here's something interesting: due to the lack of gravity, the backbones of astronauts stretch. Most astronauts become about five centimeters longer in space as a result! But don't worry: once back on Earth, they go back to their normal height.

"Hey Maya," Luke suddenly said. "I'm thirsty!" With a grin, he pulled a can of cola from his backpack.

"Oh! Me too!" Maya said eagerly.

Luke opened the can, and at once a big bubble of cola came floating out. The bubble hung in the air, wobbling around like a piece of jelly.

Maya pricked the bubble, and a big drop of cola stuck to her finger. She licked it off. "Yes," she giggled, "it tastes just like cola."

They took turns taking bites from the bubbles of cola.

"How cool would it be if we could always drink cola like this?" Luke laughed. "This is way more fun than the regular way!"

"Do you think there might be a telephone on board?" Maya wondered. "So we can call Earth?"

"Yes, of course there is!" Luke answered. "We'll just call ground control, and they'll know what to do!"

Maya and Luke wriggled through the air to get to the computer panels. All sorts of texts rolled by on the monitors.

"Do you understand any of this?" Maya asked.

"Not a word," said Luke.

"Look, over there," said Maya, and she pushed herself to the other side of the room. There was a pair of headphones. She put them on and immediately took them off again. Startled, she looked at Luke. "I heard someone!"

"That's a good thing, right? Let me try it," Luke said. He took the headphones from Maya and put them on.

A voice echoed through the headphone: "Hello, can you hear me? Hello?"

"Yes, we can hear you!" Luke answered excitedly.

A loud cheering sounded through the headphones.

Talking in space

We can communicate with astronauts on spaceships using radio waves. Since the distances in space are very large, it sometimes takes a while before a message arrives. The further away from Earth the spaceship is, the longer it takes for a message to arrive. To communicate with someone on Mars, it would take minutes before the message is received . . . So that could be a very long conversation!

The atmosphere

The **atmosphere** is the layer of air and gas around our Earth. It protects us against external dangers. For example, the atmosphere blocks small meteoroids, but also dangerous radiation. And the atmosphere also makes sure that oxygen and water don't fly into space. So, it's quite important!

"I'm Michael, the communication manager of this mission. You gave us quite a scare here at ground control. But we're glad you're all right."

Luke nodded. He couldn't speak and swallowed the lump in his throat.

Michael had a whole list of questions. What were their names? How old were they? How much did they weigh? Were they feeling sick? Weak? Nauseous? Dizzy? Normal astronauts spent years and years training for their first journey, but Luke and Maya were unprepared!

"The Mars Cruiser is operated by a special flight computer," Michael explained, after Luke had turned on the intercom. "It makes sure everything runs smoothly along the way. The thing is: it could be risky if we interrupt the computer now to get you guys back to Earth. So, we think it's safer to just continue the journey, but faster. Is that clear for you?"

"Um, not really," Luke said. "What do you mean *faster*?"

"Well . . . This space rocket is equipped with a warp drive. Do you know what that is?"

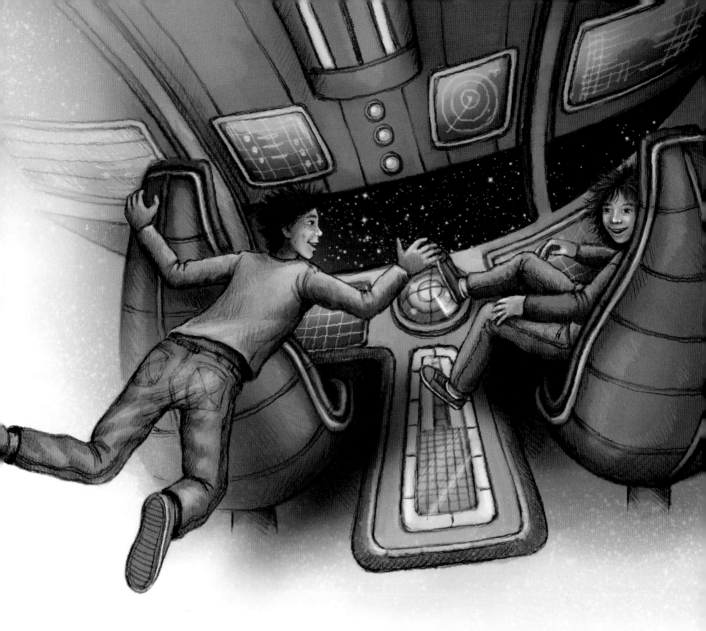

Where does space start?

"Space" begins 62 miles (one hundred kilometers) above the earth's surface. This imaginary boundary between the earth's atmosphere and space is called the Kármán line.

A warp drive is a special way to travel through space," Michael explained. "We use it to fly faster than ever before. Maybe even faster than light. Are you up for it?"

Luke and Maya looked at each other.

"Is it dangerous?" Luke asked.

"We don't know," said Michael. "We haven't had a chance to test the warp drive yet. But the trip to Mars would take months, and that's much too long and even more dangerous for you."

"So, we are really going to Mars?" Luke asked.

"Yes, if we don't diverge from the program," Michael said.

Luke's eyes were twinkling, and he looked at Maya. "This is like a real science fiction movie! We might be the first people ever on Mars!"

Michael instructed Luke and Maya to go to the cockpit and explained how to strap themselves securely into their seats. They were nervous, but gave the agreed okay sign when they were ready.

Suddenly, they heard a low humming sound. It got higher and higher, until it sounded like a singing teakettle. And the voice that counted down for the launch before, now started again: "Three . . . Two . . . One . . . Start warp drive engine."

One-way ticket to Mars

If you want to travel to Mars, it's smart to bring some snacks for the road. It's a very long journey. The distance between Mars and Earth varies: sometimes the two planets are closer together, and sometimes they're further apart. But even when Mars is closest to Earth, the distance is still about 34 million miles (56 million kilometers). It would literally take you months to get there!

Maya and Luke felt as if they were pulled into the rubber band of a catapult. The rocket shot forward like a bullet. The speed was so fast that the stars looked like long stripes. But it was deathly quiet, like being under water. After a while, there was less pressure in the cockpit. The sound returned, and Maya and Luke were able to move again.

"Congratulations," said Michael through the intercom. "You're officially the first people to travel through space at warp speed."

Luke and Maya were beaming.

"If we continue at this speed," said Michael, "we'll reach Mars in no time. In the meantime, you can enjoy the view."

Luke looked through the small windows of the cockpit. "Wow, do you see that, Maya?"

"It's so pretty," Maya said as she gazed out of the window.

"It really is," Luke said enchanted.

"Look, Luke, there's Mars!" said Maya.

Right in front of them, they saw a planet that looked a little like a rust-colored marble.

The planet in red

Mars is red because there's a thin layer of rust on its surface. The real colors of Mars are dark yellow, brown, and even a little greenish. Due to big storms that often rage over Mars, the planet looks redder than it actually is.

"We are already pretty close, right?" Luke asked.

"Yes," said Michael, "in ten minutes the computer will start to land the craft. Stay seated. The rest will happen automatically."

Slowly, the rocket turned around and began descending backwards toward Mars' surface.

But suddenly, the alarm blared. The cockpit lit up red. "Warning. Landing system error. Warning," said the computer voice.

Luke and Maya looked around in horror. "Michael, what's happening?"

"We don't know exactly, but don't worry. We're looking into it."

"Luke!" Maya said excitedly. "Do you remember the man in the coveralls?"

"You're right! I almost forgot about him."

"Michael?" Maya called.

No response.

"Michael!"

"Hang on a minute," said Michael. "We have a huge problem! Something is wrong with the communication."

"But we might know why!" Luke yelled.

"Tell me?" said Michael.

"Well . . ." Maya started to say. "Right before the launch, a man entered the Mars Cruiser. A worker, in blue coveralls and a yellow helmet. We saw him remove a panel and pull one of the electricity wires loose."

"Which panel was it?" Michael asked.

"In the cargo hold," Luke answered.

A little problem?

"Houston, we've had a problem here." That's what astronaut Jack Swigert said during his trip to the moon. An oxygen tank had exploded aboard the Apollo 13, and the trip had to be aborted. The crew came home safely, but it didn't always end that well. The crew aboard the space shuttles Challenger and Columbia were killed when something went wrong during the flight. Space travel can be dangerous, and astronauts know that.

Michael sounded alarmed.

"We will have security search for that man, but it sounds like he may have put the mission in jeopardy!"

Michael was quiet for a while.

"We need your help," he said eventually. "You'll need to make a repair, or else the landing system won't work, and you'll crash on Mars."

Luke and Maya looked back through the window. Mars was getting awfully close. They didn't have much time, that was clear. They pushed through the passageways and hatches, toward the cargo hold and the panel.

There, the red alarm lights were blinking too, and the computer voice repeated: "Warning. Landing system error. Warning."

Luke pulled the panel as hard as he could. Suddenly, the wall piece came loose, and he tumbled backwards. Quickly, he pushed himself back.

Together, they looked at all the electronics that had been hidden behind the panel. It looked impressive: lights, buttons, and a whole lot of wires and cables. Four wires were loose: two white ones, a red one, and a blue one.

"Michael, where do these wires go?" Luke yelled.

"Do you see that blue switch? That's where the blue wire needs to go. You can just click it in, you see?"

"Yes, I see," said Luke, and he fastened the blue wire.

"And the red wire in the red switch!" said Michael.

Luke's hands were still shaking. He clicked the red wire under the red switch. "But now there are two white wires left," he said nervously.

"The left wire goes left, and the right wire goes right!" Michael called through the intercom.

It was hard for Luke to tell which side the wires came from. They would just have to guess, there was no other way. He clicked one of the white wires and Maya the other.

"May the Force be with us," Luke said.

For a few seconds nothing changed. The red lights kept blinking, and the computer voice went on and on: "Warning. Landing system error. Warning."

Just when Maya and Luke thought they were doomed, the big light flashed on. The computer voice said: "Landing system restored."

Luke and Maya looked at each other a little dazedly for a second and then started cheering: "Yes! We did it! We did it!"

God of war

Most of the planets and moons in our solar system are named after Roman and Greek gods. Mars was named after the Roman god of war.

Loud cheering sounded through the intercom.

"Luke and Maya, if you hadn't been on board to discover this sabotage and to repair it, the Mars Cruiser would've crashed, and the entire mission would've failed. Not only did you save your own lives, but also the mission *and* the Mars Cruiser! You're heroes!"

Luke and Maya were beaming with pride.

"But please return to your seats. Because thanks to you, the first manned spaceship is landing on Mars."

Luke and Maya floated back to the cockpit and fastened their seatbelts.

Mars was now so close they could see the surface: orange mountain ridges, copper-colored deserts, and in the distance a pole with a paper-thin layer of ice on top.

They landed with a violent thud on the ground.

"NASA must've never heard of shock absorbers," Maya said sharply.

"You're now free to walk around in the Mars Cruiser," said Michael. "But careful, because the gravity on Mars is a lot weaker than on Earth. Meanwhile, we'll prepare the Mars Cruiser for the return journey."

Luke thought for a minute. "Michael, can we ask for a favor?"

"Of course, Luke."

"I would really like to walk on Mars with Maya!"

It was quiet for a while on the other end of the intercom. "Well, we would be violating a lot of protocols, but you did save the mission, so if you promise to do exactly as I say, we can make that happen."

The next moment, Maya and Luke were putting on spacesuits. In the hoods of the spacesuits were a microphone and a loudspeaker, so they could still talk to each other *and* to Michael.

They walked toward the air lock.

"Now press that big button, and enter the air lock," Michael said. "The door will close automatically behind you."

There was another button next to a second door. Maya pressed it, and this one opened as well. They saw the rust-colored landscape of Mars appear before them.

Maya and Luke stepped out into a desert of orange sand. Every step looked like a ballet leap. Maya was dancing around with big, graceful jumps. She did pirouettes and gracefully stretched her arms.

Meanwhile, Luke was looking at his own footprints. Their footprints were the first human footprints on Mars.

Maya stopped and looked in the distance. "Luke, do you see that?"

Orange-colored clouds appeared on the horizon. They looked threatening.

"You two have to go back to the Mars Cruiser *right now*," Michael said tensely. "That's a sandstorm, and it's approaching quickly!"

Water

Is there water on Mars? The surface of the planet looks dry and bare, but there are indications that there used to be rivers and lakes there. Mars has a thinner atmosphere than Earth, and maybe that's why the water has evaporated and disappeared into space. But it's also possible that some of the water has fallen into the ground and has frozen there. Scientists want to know what happened to the water on Mars. Because Mars and Earth are so similar, we might learn more about our planet. And if there's water on Mars, then there may be life as well.

Maya and Luke ran back to the Mars Cruiser with big jumps and quickly climbed on board.

As the sandstorm roared passed them, the Mars Cruiser shook and trembled.

"It looks like more sandstorms are on the way," said Michael. "We'll prepare to leave now."

Maya and Luke wriggled out of the spacesuits and jumped back into the cargo hold as quickly as possible, while the computer was counting down for departure. They hurried to their seats, strapped their seatbelts, and a second later, the spaceship shot in the air.

From space, the sandstorms looked innocent: a soft, orange mist over a rusty surface.

Dust storms

Mars has the biggest sandstorms in our solar system. These dust storms can become so big that you can see them from Earth (with a telescope at least). Sometimes, a storm is so large that it covers all of Mars.

The return trip had started.

"I loved visiting Mars," said Maya, "but I did miss the green of the trees and the blue of the ocean. I prefer Earth."

"Yes, and the oxygen and the gravity on Earth are pretty nice too," Luke agreed.

"And how about pancakes?" Maya beamed.

"Oh yes!" Luke said. He was starving. "Once we get back to Earth, I want pancakes with syrup!"

Then Michael's voice sounded through the intercom again: "Guys, we are approaching Earth. Get ready, because we are entering the atmosphere at an incredible speed. It's going to be a rough landing!"

Luke and Maya looked through the window to Earth. It was a beautiful blue-green ball with nice white clouds. From a distance, it looked vulnerable and small.

"Isn't that crazy?" said Luke. "That everyone and everything you love lives on that one tiny ball in space?"

"It sure is," said Maya.

The landing had started, and Michael didn't lie. Shaking and trembling, the rocket shot through the atmosphere. The nose of the Mars Cruiser appeared to be burning and blazing due to friction with the atmosphere. Gradually, the spaceship was slowing down. Like a big plane, the Mars Cruiser flew toward the runway in Florida. With a few loud bumps, the spacecraft landed on its wheels. It needed the whole runway to slow down and reach a standstill. But it worked!

Luke and Maya loosened their seatbelts and hurried to the air lock. The door opened, and outside a crowd of people was waiting for them. There was loud clapping and cheering, and pictures were taken.

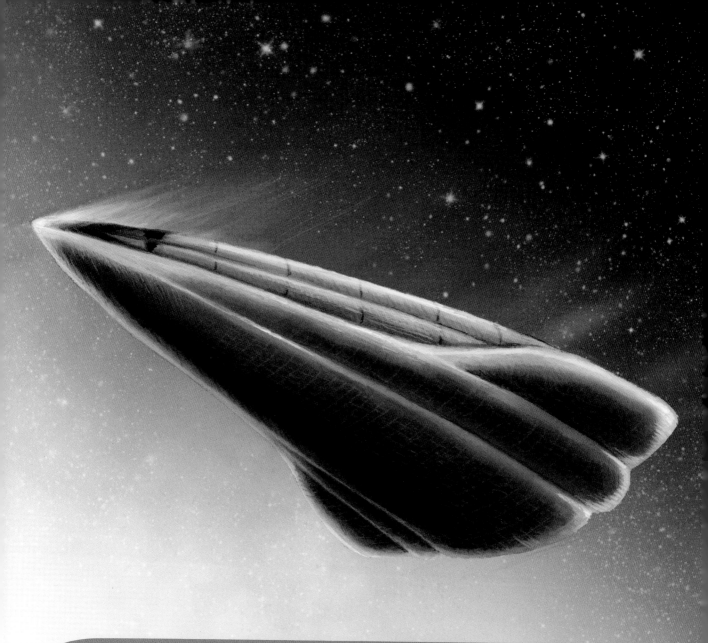

Bursting into the atmosphere

When a spacecraft comes back to Earth, it must penetrate the earth's atmosphere, where it encounters friction with the air. This friction makes it very hot, and without protection, the spacecraft would burn. That's why spaceships are equipped with heat shields.

"Luke! Luke!" someone called. "Luke! Wake up!"

Luke opened his eyes and immediately squinted against the bright light. To his surprise, he was lying in bed, with the Space Fighter in his arms. "Maya?" he croaked sleepily. "But weren't we . . ."

Maya looked at him with a questioning look. "I just came in. You were snoring really loudly!"

"Oh . . ." Luke looked around him. "But it all felt so real! We were on Mars together, and there was a sandstorm."

Maya looked at Luke with her head cocked. "You're just upset that you came in second place. Come on, let's go get something to eat. I'm hungry," said Maya.

"Me too," said Luke. "I could really eat some pancakes with a lot of syrup!"

He got up and left the Space Fighter on his bed.

Together, they walked out of Luke's bedroom. Not noticing they left a trail of red-colored sand on the carpet.

Table of contents

File:
The Universe

Ready for the biggest secrets of our cosmos?

1
The beginning of everything

How did the universe come into being? No one really knows. After all, it happened a long time ago, and we can't travel back in time to take a look. Yet, scientists have been trying to unravel the mysteries of the universe for centuries.

The Big Bang

The best-known theory about the origin of the universe is probably the **Big Bang theory**. It says that the entire universe was once compressed into a very tiny ball, even smaller than a pinhead. That so-called **primeval atom** would've exploded, and all matter of the universe would've been thrown around in the process.

Blowing firmly

You can compare the creation of the universe with the idea of blowing up a balloon: at first, it's small, but it gets bigger and bigger. Even now, the universe continues to expand in all directions, like a balloon that's being inflated more and more.

Silent bang

According to some scientists, the Big Bang didn't make any noise at all. Sound requires air, which did not exist at the time.

13.8 billion
years ago:
the Big Bang

13.4 billion years ago:
the first stars
were born

4.7 billion years ago:
our solar system begins

0 seconds ago:
the universe as
it is now

One big soup

After the Big Bang, the universe was a burning hot mixture of particles, substances, gasses, and light. This mixture is called the **primordial soup**. Stars and planets only came into being when that mess started to clump together, which lasted hundreds of millions of years.

Not really tasty . . .
But was this what the
primordial soup
looked like?

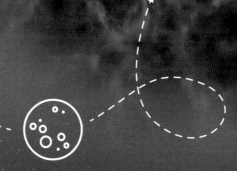

And before that?

There seems to be a lot of truth in the Big Bang theory, but it doesn't explain everything. For example, it's still unclear what happened before the Big Bang. Maybe there were other universes, and our universe arose from them. Or maybe the Big Bang was the beginning of everything and therefore also of time. Nobody really knows for sure.

2

Our solar system

*Welcome to our solar system! A **solar system** is a big star with all kinds of celestial bodies rotating around it. In our solar system, there are countless boulders and stones floating around, but also eight real planets.*

Mercury

A **planet** is a celestial body that moves around a star. Mercury, Venus, Earth, and Mars are four small and rocky planets. They're called the **terrestrial planets**, because they have a surface of solids.

Mars

Olympus Mons is located on Mars: this is the largest volcano in our solar system.

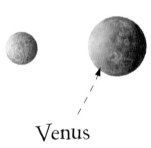

Venus

A planet with a mind of its own! All other planets in our solar system rotate in an easterly direction, but Venus rotates in a westerly direction.

The Earth
That's the planet you live on!

The sun

Our **sun** is a **star**. Actually, the words sun and star have the exact same meaning: a luminous celestial body.

Jupiter

Jupiter and Saturn are called **gas giants**: they're large planets, which consist mainly of gas.

Kuiper belt

A band of blocks of stone and ice, right on the edge of our solar system.

Saturn

The only planet with clearly visible rings. These consist of particles of ice and stone.

asteroid belt

A wide belt of rocks flying around.

Uranus

Uranus and Neptune are **ice giants**. They're smaller than Jupiter and Saturn, but larger than the terrestrial planets.

And what about Pluto?

Pluto was long regarded as the ninth planet of our solar system. But actually, it's too small for that. That's why it's no longer called a planet, but a dwarf planet.

Neptune

This blue planet is named after the Roman god of the sea.

3

The earth and the moon

Our Earth and our moon. Of course, you already know those big celestial bodies.
But surely, you don't know everything about them . . .

Our Earth is a hothead

Earth hasn't always been the blue-green sphere it is today. The planet took shape when gas, dust, and debris from the primordial soup started to stick together. At that time, it was still a hot bulb with fire, volcanoes, and swirling lava. It took a long time before the outer layer started to cool down and form a hard crust.

The mantle
A thick layer of hard rock under the earth's crust.

The earth's crust
The outer, hard layer of the earth.

The outer core
A swirling mass of sweltering hot lava.

The inner core
A fixed sphere in the middle of the earth.

The atmosphere
A layer of air and gas around the earth.

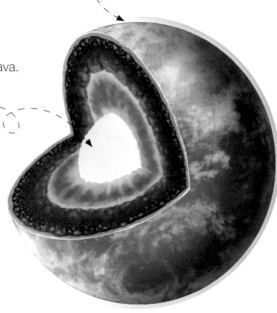

Inside out

**Want to see for yourself how hot it is inside the earth?
Then take a look
at a volcanic eruption!**

Our moon

This is the moon. It's *our* moon, but it surely isn't the only one. A **moon** is a celestial body circling around a planet (or other boulders, like a dwarf planet). Earth has one moon. But Mars has two. And boaster Jupiter even has 79!

How do you make a moon?

Some scientists think that our moon came into being because a huge boulder collided with the Earth a long time ago. It is said that a large part of our planet was broken down, and that later became the moon.

Attention! Attention!
How do you tell the difference between a planet and a moon? A planet revolves around a star, and a moon revolves around a planet.

Moon month

The moon revolves around our Earth. Each round takes about a month. That's where the word "month" comes from.

The moon shines through the trees

People sometimes say that the moon is shining, but actually that's not true. The moon itself doesn't give light: it only reflects the light from the sun. Because the moon rotates around the earth, we don't always see as many sunrays falling on it: sometimes we see a full moon, sometimes a crescent moon, sometimes a sickle. We call this a **phase**. The moon always remains a sphere. It only seems to change its shape.

4

The sun

Nice and hot, that sun of ours. And interesting!

Baby stars

In our universe, there are huge clouds of gas and dust floating around. And in these so-called **nebulae**, stars are born. Hundreds and hundreds of stars. That's why nebulae are also called **stellar nurseries**.

Fusspot

A star is formed when the gas in a nebula contracts and forms a very dense ball of gas. When the pressure becomes strong enough, chemical reactions take place that cause the sphere to emit light and heat. And . . . a star is born!

Life of a star

Stars resemble living creatures: they are born, exist for a while, and die again. When a star grows older, it slowly warms up more and more. This takes billions of years. It also becomes brighter and bigger, until it changes into an enormous red star: a so-called **red giant**. Afterwards, it loses its outer layers, and only a small white point remains. This **white dwarf** is almost as big as the earth and continues to glow for billions of years.

Do you remember?
A star is a celestial body that gives light.

Our sun in numbers

- Age: 4.6 billion years

- Distance to the Earth: 93 million miles (150 million kilometers)

- Diameter: 864.340 miles (1.4 million kilometers) (that's 109 Earth globes in a row)

- Temperature on the surface: 9.941 degrees Fahrenheit (5.500 degrees Celsius)

- Temperature in the core: 27 million degrees Fahrenheit (15 million degrees Celsius)

Not all stars shine . . .

When you look at a star, sometimes it seems as if it radiates. But that's not really the case. It's because we have little wrinkles on the retinae of our eyes. Those wrinkles refract the light and make it seem as if the stars radiate.

Rocks flying around

In the universe, there are many kinds of rocks flying around.

Orbiting rocks

Planetoids or **asteroids** are rocks orbiting the sun, but they're too small to be called "planets." Most asteroids in our solar system race around in the asteroid belt. Some rocks are as small as grains of sand, while others have a diameter of more than a thousand kilometers.

Failed!

Some scientists think that a planet should've been born out of the rocks in the asteroid belt, but Jupiter prevented it. Jupiter's gravitational force was so strong that it was able to keep the rocks apart so they couldn't cluster, as happened with the other planets. So, the asteroid belt might be a failed planet.

Do you remember?
The asteroid belt is a wide belt of rocks flying around between Mars and Jupiter.

Space snowball

A **comet** is a ball of ice and dust. It's recognizable by its tail. The tail develops when a comet passes the sun and the ice evaporates and changes into gas. The sunlight radiates against the wisps of gas and makes it seem as if the comet has a tail.

Hello Halley!

The best-known comet is Halley's comet. From Earth, you can see it once every 76 years. Write it down on your calendar: in 2061, Halley will pass the earth again!

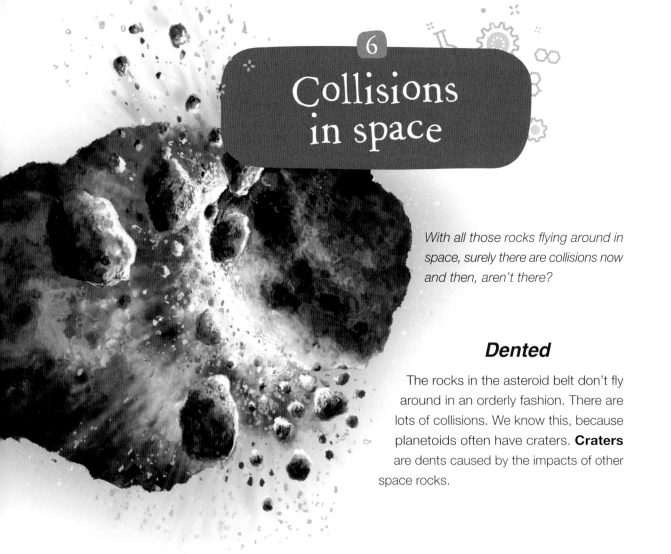

6

Collisions in space

With all those rocks flying around in space, surely there are collisions now and then, aren't there?

Dented

The rocks in the asteroid belt don't fly around in an orderly fashion. There are lots of collisions. We know this, because planetoids often have craters. **Craters** are dents caused by the impacts of other space rocks.

Protective shield

The earth is surrounded by the **atmosphere**, a layer of air and gas, that functions as a shield. Most of the rocks racing towards the earth globe are burned before they reach us.

Rubbing out

When a rock does crash against the earth, it creates a crater. Over thousands and thousands of years, the craters begin to wash away by rain, hail, ice, and wind. This is called **erosion**. It's not the same for all celestial bodies. The moon, for example, doesn't have an atmosphere. That's why the craters on the moon stay visible forever.

Meteoroids
Little pieces of stone in space that we can't see from the Earth.

Meteors
Meteoroids entering the atmosphere.

Meteorites
Pieces of meteors falling on Earth. This happens very rarely.

Bye, bye, dinosaurs!

Some scientists think dinosaurs are extinct because of a gigantic meteorite crash. The crash caused an enormous dust cloud, blocking out the sunlight. Thus, the Earth became dark and cold, plants couldn't grow anymore, and dinosaurs starved and eventually died.

7

Explosions in space

There are many types of explosions, bursts, and eruptions in space . . .

Novae

When a small star and a big star hang about close together, the first one sometimes steals some gas and energy from the latter one. Sometimes more than it can digest, and then an explosion takes place: a **nova**.

Gamma-ray bursts

The heaviest bangs in space? **Gamma-ray bursts.** Those are hundreds of times more powerful than supernovae. They come into being by the melting together of stars. Luckily, we see them only at a huge distance.

Fast radio bursts

Superfast! **Fast radio bursts** are very short explosions. They only take a fraction of a second. They take place everywhere in space, but nobody knows how they come into being. Mysterious!

Supernovae

A supernova is even more forceful than a plain nova. (That's why it's called supernova, of course.) A **supernova** can come into being when a small star steals energy from a big star and then explodes. When a very large star has been burned down inside and collapses, setting free so much energy, it also explodes immediately.

8

The Milky Way

Almost everything you can see in space with the naked eye is part of the Milky Way. But what's the Milky Way?

A trail of milk?

The **Milky Way**. That's the name of the galaxy we live in. A **galaxy** is a territory in space with a large number of stars. The Milky Way, for example, consists of billions of stars that are surrounded by dust clouds, gases, planets, moons, planetoids, and comets. Seen from Earth, the Milky Way looks like a stripe in the universe. That stripe is not tight and straight, but a little splotchy. As if a trail of milk has been spilled!

Attention! Attention!
With so many stars, you might think the Milky Way is very crowded. But no: the Milky Way is so huge that all stars are at enormous distances from one another.

Egg

According to some people, the Milky Way looks like an egg sunny-side up, because in the middle there's a hump (called the **central bulge**) that looks like an egg yolk.

From a small distance

From Earth, the Milky Way appears like a stripe in space. But that's because we're in the middle of it. From a small distance, the Milky Way looks like a flat disk with four big and several smaller spiral arms. Earth is dangling somewhere in the Orion arm, one of the smaller arms.

9

Other galaxies

For a long time, people thought the Milky Way was the only galaxy in the universe. Ha-ha!
Now we know there are billions of them!

Local Group

Our Milky Way is part of a group of galaxies that's called the Local Group: a group of more than forty galaxies.

A large group of stars
is called a **galaxy**.

But galaxies themselves often group together.
Those we call **clusters**.

The clusters form larger bands,
called **superclusters**.

And the superclusters gather together
in even larger networks, called **filaments**.

All shapes and sizes

There are galaxies in all kinds of forms, but the most common are:

Elliptical galaxies:
spherical to elongated

Disc galaxies:
flat pancakes with
spiral arms

Irregular galaxies:
without recognizable form

Cannibals!

When a large galaxy and a small galaxy come near to each other, sometimes things go wrong. The large galaxy will pull the smaller one to itself . . . and devour it! That could take billions of years, so it's not exactly a quick bite.

10

Exoplanets

Our galaxy has eight planets.
But in the universe, there are lots and lots more.
What about them?

Exoplanet

An **exoplanet** is a planet turning around a star other than
the sun. In other words: a planet out of our solar system.
There's a huge number of stars in the universe, and so
there are lots and lots of exoplanets.

Bling bling

Most well-known exoplanets don't resemble our Earth. Sometimes, they're
ice planets or gas giants. But also a pink and a black exoplanet have
been discovered. And one that consists almost fully out of water.
And even one that's made mostly of diamond!

Far away neighbor

Proxima Centauri b. That's the
exoplanet closest to Earth. But even
this one is at an enormous distance:
literally trillions of miles away.

Do you remember?
The eight planets of our solar
system are: Mercury, Venus,
Earth, Mars, Jupiter, Saturn,
Uranus, and Neptune.

Habitable zone

Is there life on the exoplanets? Life can only come into being on planets that are at exactly the right distance from their star: too close and everything will burn down, too far and everything will freeze. The zone in between those areas, where life is possible, is called the **habitable zone**.

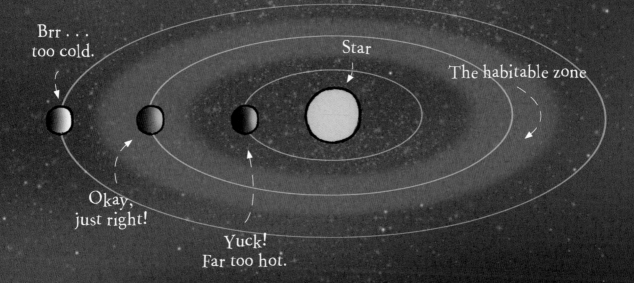

Brr . . .
too cold.

Star

The habitable zone

Okay,
just right!

Yuck!
Far too hot.

The habitable zone is also called the **Goldilocks zone**, because the habitable zone is not too hot and not too cold, but just right.

How to find an exoplanet

Exoplanets are hard to find, because they're so far away.
And they don't give light . . . Still, clever ways have been found to detect them.

The Doppler technique

Stars and planets have gravitational force: they "pull" one another, as if they would like to be nearer. That's why, when a planet turns around a star, the star wobbles a little. Thus, scientists know: when a star moves, there may be a planet nearby.

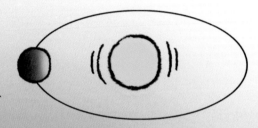

The transit method

A star shines. The light becomes less bright when a planet passes in front of the star. Just as a desk lamp gets darker when you hold a tennis ball in front of it. When a star gives less light, this may signify a planet passing by.

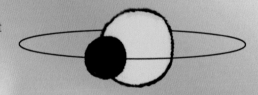

A picture postcard
from Kepler-452b

Does the exoplanet look like this?

Exoplanet hunters

*Luckily, we don't have to look for exoplanets ourselves.
Equipment does this for us.*

The Kepler space telescope

The Kepler space telescope used the transit method to discover exoplanets. For years, it looked at specific stars and sent information about them to Earth. In that way, thousands of exoplanets have been discovered.

Never really sure

Nobody knows exactly what exoplanets look like. They're simply too far away to explore. There are only drawings of what we think exoplanets might look like.

The TESS

The TESS (Transiting Exoplanet Survey Satellite) functions almost the same way as the Kepler space telescope. But it doesn't focus on one part of the Milky Way. It looks in all directions. Thus, it can see a lot more.

Extraterrestrial life

Aliens, Martians, extraterrestrial beings . . . Is Earth unique, or are there other planets with living beings?

Vivid imagination

People love to daydream about extraterrestrial beings. But do aliens really exist, or are they just in our imaginations?

Good things come in small packages

Maybe extraterrestrials are large creatures, like humans. But there could be microscopic small beings too, like microbes.

Space tardigrades

An experiment! Scientists once sent a couple of tardigrades into space. These animals are extremely tiny, but also extremely strong. The experiment made this clear: humans cannot survive in space one single minute without a special outfit, but the tardigrades stayed alive for more than ten days. This proves there could be life in environments completely different from those we're accustomed to.

Clever

Some scientists are searching for intelligent extraterrestrial life: aliens just as clever as we are, or even more intelligent! This kind of research is called SETI: Search for Extraterrestrial Intelligence. For example, the SETI Institute in California does this kind of research.

A tardigrade!
But enormously blown up, because in reality, it's only half a millimeter small.

Interview with Seth Shostak

Astronomer at the SETI Institute

How do you search for extraterrestrial life?

"Normally we use large radio antennae. They look like normal saucer antennae, but they're a lot bigger. Large enough to receive radio emissions from other worlds. That's difficult, because the signals have to cover huge distances and are probably very weak."

Is there life on Mars?

"I hope so! Billions of years ago, Mars was more suitable for life than it is now, with oceans and a better atmosphere. Maybe back then there was microscopic life. And maybe that life disappeared underground, when Mars slowly ran dry. But we just don't know."

Have there ever been aliens on Earth?

"I don't think so. Lots of people claim they've seen flying saucers or aliens . . . But if we had ever been visited by extraterrestrial beings, we would have some proof."

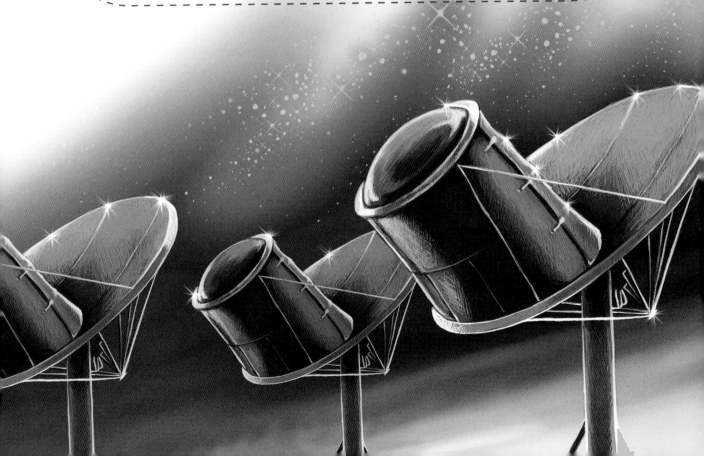

14

But then . . . where are they?

Maybe there's extraterrestrial life . . . But then why are we still not sure about it?

Where?

The universe is very, very old and very, very large. There are many, many stars and many, many planets . . . So you might expect there are lots of extraterrestrial beings. But we've never found any proof of their existence. No aliens, no spaceships, no radio signals. In other words: if extraterrestrial beings exist, then where are they?

Paradox

This question is called the **Fermi paradox**, because it was physicist Enrico Fermi who posed it so clearly for the first time. A **paradox** is a seeming antithesis. In this case, the expected presence of lots of extraterrestrial life doesn't seem to match the absolute absence of evidence.

Three possible reasons why we still don't have any evidence:

We live too far away

The universe is huge. Maybe we're just too far away from other living creatures, and maybe that's the reason why we still haven't found them.

We haven't been searching long enough yet

People have always been looking at the skies, but space shuttles and telescopes are recent inventions. We haven't had a lot of time to search yet.

We've been looking in the wrong places

We did our best, but maybe we've just been searching in the wrong spots all the time.

Wow!

In 1977, the American astronomer Jerry R. Ehman captures a very special signal from space. Maybe it's a message from extraterrestrial life! But because the signal had been received only once, nobody could determine what it was exactly. When Ehman detected this particular signal, he wrote down "Wow!" on his papers. That's why the signal has been called the **Wow! signal**.

15

Big questions about the universe

There's a lot to be discovered about space. Some things we know already, others stay mysterious. Do you know the answers to the following questions?

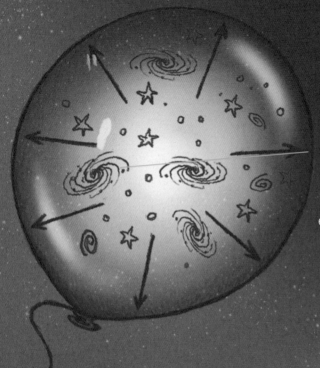

What's dark energy?

As the universe expands, it gets bigger and bigger, and the expansion happens more and more quickly. Scientists don't understand how this is possible. That's why they invented **dark energy**: a mysterious power permeating the whole universe, pushing everything apart.

What's dark matter?

From the chair you're sitting on to the book you're holding, everything is made out of something. We call this: **matter**. You could say: matter is everything you can see and grab. But scientists think there's also another kind of matter.

When they were exploring faraway galaxies, they were unable to find eighty percent of the matter. So perhaps there's a kind of matter we cannot see or grab: **dark matter**.

What are gravitational waves?

Imagine two heavy objects, like stars, turning around
each other. Those stars have a strong gravitational force,
but because of their movements, the location changes all the
time. This causes small waves in the universe. Because of these
so-called **gravitational waves**, everything in space wobbles a little.

What are black holes?

In some spots in the universe, the gravitational force is so strong that it attracts everything.
Even light cannot escape! Those are **black
holes** you cannot see, literally. Scientists are
exploring black holes by looking at the stars
around them. They're evident, because their
light is being sucked away.

What's stardust?

Stardust or **cosmic dust** consists of very small particles floating through space. The dust
contains all physical basic ingredients that everything in the universe is made off: stars, planets, animals . . . and humans. Yes, you too are made of stardust!

16

More big questions about the universe

Is the universe endless?

Nobody knows exactly how big the universe is. Scientists can't even see it completely. Some stars are so far away their light hasn't even reached us yet. The part that we can see is called the observable universe. We know that outside of this there's more, but we don't know how much more.

Why is the universe black?

The universe is colorless, because it's so empty. We can only see colors when light hits an object and the rays are reflected to our eyes. But if the sunlight hits nothing, everything appears black.

What's a parallel universe?

Imagine if our universe had a twin, a second universe just like ours, or perhaps a little different. That second universe is called a **parallel universe**, because "parallel" means "similar." Parallel universes often appear in science fiction.

Is there a Planet X?

At the outskirts of our solar system, there's a strip of floating bits of rock and ice. Some rocks in this Kuiper belt behave a little strangely: their orbit around the sun is different than expected. According to some scientists, this is caused by an unknown planet which is even further away from the sun. The gravitational force of this **Planet X** might be causing the unusual behavior of the rocky pieces. But other scientists believe this is nonsense and think the rocks are just colliding. Who knows?

According to some theories, our universe is not the only one. There might be more universes. Maybe an infinite number. All those universes together are called the **multiverse**.

17

And even more big questions about the universe

maximum speed
186.282 miles
(300.000 kilometers)
per second!

Can we travel faster than light?

Whoosh! Light travels at about 186.282 miles (300.000 kilometers) per second. According to physicists, nothing is faster than light. And it's impossible for humans to travel at the speed of light. But who knows, maybe we can do it in the future!

What's a warp drive?

Sorry! But a **warp drive** doesn't really exist. It was invented by the makers of the science fiction series *Star Trek*. They wanted their characters to be able to travel through space really fast, so they invented this fake technology.

What's a wormhole?

A **wormhole** is a shortcut: a kind of tunnel in space, changing and shortening the distance between two places. It takes less time to travel from one spot to the other. According to the calculations of a lot of scientists, wormholes could exist, but the likelihood is rather small.

Does time travel exist?

Do you ever dream of visiting the Middle Ages or having a space holiday in the future? Alas, this type of **time travel** only exists in movies and books. There are scientists who think a lot about time travel, but according to them, you would have to be able to be faster than light, get around a black hole, or tumble through a wormhole . . . All those things aren't within reach . . . yet!

What's the color of the sun?

White. The sun only appears to be yellow, because the rays have to travel through the atmosphere.

What's a Dyson sphere?

Is it possible to capture all solar energy from a star? Maybe with the help of a **Dyson sphere**: an enormous shell built around a star. In order to encompass a complete celestial body this way, you would need a megastructure or a lot of smaller structures that fit together as a jigsaw. However, for the moment, a structure like that is nothing but science fiction.

18

The universe and the zodiac

The universe is full of pictures.
But you have to use your imagination in order to see them.

Drawing with stars

The **astrological signs** were invented long ago. At that time, there was no street lighting, so the starry sky was really visible at night. People looked up, drew imaginative lines between the stars, and saw pictures come into being.

Pleased to meet you!

This is Claudius Ptolemy, a Greek scientist who lived from the year 87 to the year 168. He made an early list of astrological signs. A lot of them are still used today.

Celestial zoo

The most well-known astrological signs are the signs of the **zodiac**. The zodiac is the ring of constellations that the sun seems to pass through each year while the earth orbits around it.

What are they named after?

A lot of astrological signs have been named after animals. There's Big Dipper (Great Bear), Aries (the Ram), Taurus (the Bull), Cancer (the Crab), and Pisces (the Fish). Others have been named after mythological figures: Hercules, Dragon, and Unicorn. Or even after objects: the Scales, the Arrow, and the Telescope.

Astrology

Astrology also makes use of the zodiac. Some people believe that one's future can be predicted based on the astrological signs. But astrology is not a science.

Aquarius (Waterman)

Pisces (Fish)

Aries (Ram)

Taurus (Bull)

Gemini (Twins)

Cancer (Crab)

Capricorn (Goat)

Leo (Lion)

Sagittarius (Archer)

Scorpio (Scorpion)

Libra (Scales)

Virgo (Virgin)

19

The universe and science fiction

Here are five icons of science fiction.

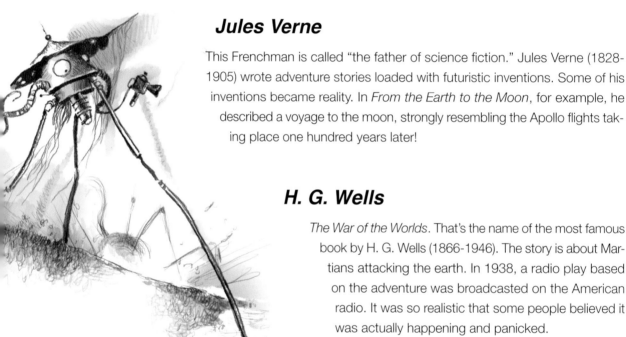

Jules Verne

This Frenchman is called "the father of science fiction." Jules Verne (1828-1905) wrote adventure stories loaded with futuristic inventions. Some of his inventions became reality. In *From the Earth to the Moon*, for example, he described a voyage to the moon, strongly resembling the Apollo flights taking place one hundred years later!

H. G. Wells

The War of the Worlds. That's the name of the most famous book by H. G. Wells (1866-1946). The story is about Martians attacking the earth. In 1938, a radio play based on the adventure was broadcasted on the American radio. It was so realistic that some people believed it was actually happening and panicked.

Carl Sagan

Astronomer Carl Sagan (1934-1966) is world-famous because of the informative television program *Cosmos* and the novel *Contact*. But also because of his idea to send recorded messages into space with the Voyager space probe. Sagan hoped extraterrestrial beings would listen to them.

George Méliès

Maybe you've never heard of George Méliès (1861-1938), but this French magician made the first science fiction movie ever. The black and white movie *A Trip to the Moon* is about a group of people landing on the moon in a kind of bullet rocket. The story was inspired by the works of Jules Verne and H. G. Wells.

George Lucas

May the Force be with you. That famous sentence comes from *Star Wars*, the movie series created by director George Lucas (1944-). Whether it's the Stormtroopers, Jedi, Star Fighters, or Darth Vader: everybody knows something about this movie series.

20

Famous astronomers

Looking back in time, there's a lot we can learn from some of the greatest astronomers in history.

Aristarchus of Samos
(310 - 230 BC)

For a long time, people thought the earth was the center of the universe. But the Greek thinker Aristarchus of Samos thought the earth was turning around the sun and not vice versa. He was way ahead of his time.

Nicolaus Copernicus
(1473 - 1543)

Nicolaus Copernicus was able to prove what Aristarchus believed: the earth is turning around the sun! But in those days, it was still a revolutionary idea, so Copernicus published a book about it just before he died.

Galileo Galilei
(1564 - 1642)

Galileo Galilei is called "the father of modern astronomy." He used a telescope to look at the sky and discovered things you can't see with the naked eye, like craters on the moon.

Johannes Kepler
(1571 - 1630)

A lot of astronomers thought planets made perfect circles around the sun. But Johannes Kepler knew better: their orbits are elliptical, causing them to be a little further or a little nearer to the sun at times.

Christiaan Huygens
(1629 - 1695)

As an astronomer, Christiaan Huygens is known (among other things) for refining the lens of a telescope. With his advanced telescope, he was able to discover the moon Titus, orbiting Saturn.

Isaac Newton
(1643 - 1727)

Bang! A famous story about Isaac Newton is that he was sitting under an apple tree, when suddenly an apple fell on his head. That's how he started thinking about gravitation and other forces in the universe.

Albert Einstein
(1879 - 1955)

Albert Einstein is known as one of the greatest thinkers of all time. Because of Einstein's theories, we know more than ever about light particles, light speed, atoms, gravitational waves, and much more.

Edwin Hubble
(1889 - 1953)

A century ago, most astronomers thought the universe consisted of one big galaxy: the Milky Way. But no! Edwin Hubble found out that there are lots of galaxies.

21

Exploring the universe

It's fun to look up at the universe on a clear night.
But it takes more if you want to make new discoveries.

Inhuman

Why is it so difficult for human beings to travel to space? Because space is completely different from the surroundings we're used to. Humans need gravity, oxygen, air pressure, sunlight, food, and water to survive. All those things are lacking in space.

Devices

Some places in the universe are too dangerous or too far away for people. But they aren't too far away for devices like Mars vehicles, space probes, telescopes, and satellites. Scientists can learn about places far off in space while staying safely on Earth.

Space robots

Human astronauts have only visited the moon. But robots have visited Mars, Jupiter, Titan, Venus, Saturn, and Pluto already. And the Voyager space probes have even left our solar system!

Intelligent robots

What's the ideal astronaut? According to some scientists, it would be an intelligent robot. Not a device being operated from Earth, but a robot that can think for itself and make its own decisions. We call this artificial intelligence.

Space holiday

On holiday in space! More and more commercial space travel companies want to send clients off to space. For the moment, it's about trips to the outskirts of the atmosphere, but in the future, you may be able to travel to other planets!

22

Telescopes on Earth

Large telescopes are important devices for exploring the universe. Because by watching and listening, astronomers can discover more and more about space.

Two kinds of large telescopes

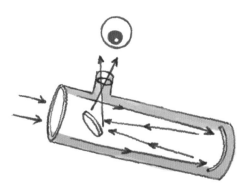

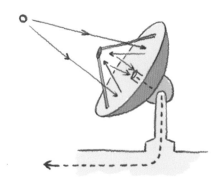

Optical telescopes are devices enabling you to see the universe. Using a clever system with lenses and mirrors, light rays are transformed, so you can see very far away.

Radio telescopes are devices enabling you to listen to the universe. They receive radio waves from space that you cannot hear with the naked ear.

> ### Do you remember?
> *The atmosphere is a layer of air and gas around the earth.*

A home for a telescope?

Almost all large telescopes are high up in the mountains, where the atmosphere is thin and where not many people live. There's a good reason for that. Optical telescopes are troubled by the atmosphere. Clouds and vibrations in the air sometimes blur the view. And in order to observe the universe really well, it should be dark. But due to all artificial lighting in crowded areas even at night, it's very bright. For radio telescopes, it's important that there are no electrical devices around: mobile phones, radios, or televisions. Those gadgets send out all kinds of signals, and these can disturb the telescope.

Big, bigger, biggest!

With telescopes, you may say: the bigger, the better. The larger the mirror that's inside, the further in space you can see. The largest mirror telescope in the world, the Gran Telescopio Canarias, has a mirror measuring 34 feet (10.4 meters). But an even larger one is already in the making: the Extremely Large Telescope will have a mirror measuring 128 feet (39 meters)!

Greek viewer

The word **"telescope"** is from the Greek roots *"tele"* meaning "far" and *"skopos"* meaning "seeing."

Dutch viewer

Did you know the telescope is a Dutch invention? We know it happened in 1608, but we're not sure who invented it.

23

Space telescopes and satellites

You can study the universe using devices on Earth.
But you can do it using devices in space too!

Satellites

People have sent all kinds of technological devices into space. There, they're orbiting the earth and other celestial bodies. We call these devices **satellites**. Some satellites play a role in facilitating our communication and navigation systems, other satellites help us study the universe.

Hubble Space Telescope

Sputnik 1

The first

Sputnik 1. That's the first satellite. The unmanned Russian device orbited the earth for three months, before burning down in the atmosphere. After this first satellite was sent into space, many others followed. Not only by Russia and the United States, but by a lot of other countries too.

A clear-cut view

The most famous space telescope is the Hubble Space Telescope. It's orbiting the earth and can see very far into the universe. It makes sharp and detailed photographs, but now better technology exists, so a successor is being developed: the James Webb Space Telescope will be launched in 2021.

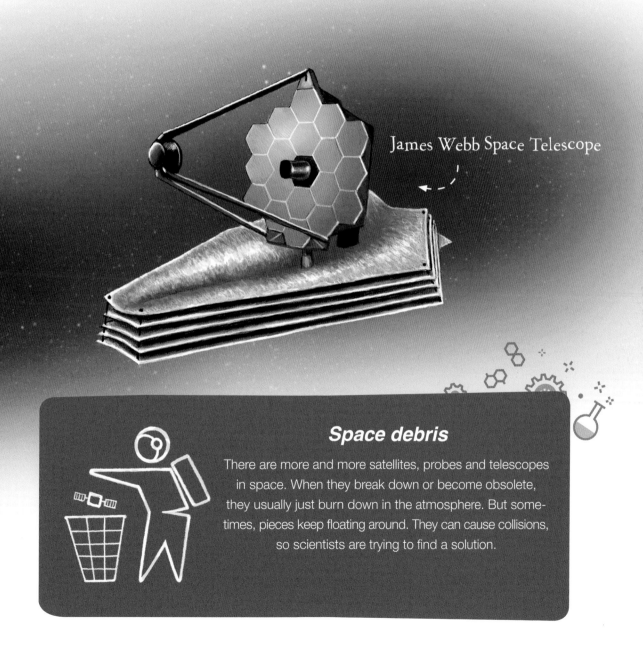

James Webb Space Telescope

Space debris

There are more and more satellites, probes and telescopes in space. When they break down or become obsolete, they usually just burn down in the atmosphere. But sometimes, pieces keep floating around. They can cause collisions, so scientists are trying to find a solution.

24

Animals in space

The first astronauts? They weren't human . . . They were animals!

Laboratory animal

In the beginning of space travel, nobody knew what
the effect of a space voyage would be. Could human
beings stand the forces of a blast-off? Would they survive a
return into the atmosphere? And would a body function without gravity? All those things had to be tested. That's why scientists sent all kinds of
animals into space, to see what happened to them. Now, when animals travel to
space, there's always someone to take care of them.

Space animals

- In 1947, the first animals travelled into space: fruit flies.

- In 1957, the first mammal went into space. Sadly, Laika, a dog, didn't survive the trip. But her successors Belka and Strelka came back home safely.

- In 1961, a chimpanzee named Ham went up. He had learned a small task to perform in space. That way, scientists could see that it was possible to work during a space voyage.

- In 1963, a little cat, Félicette, was sent into space. The animal came back safely after a parachute landing.

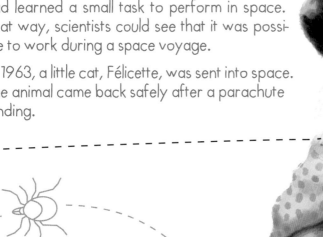

Space zoo

Lots of small animals have made a space voyage. From cockroaches to spiders, from turtles to mice, from frogs and beetles to shrimps and bees, and from ants to silkworms.

Animal rights!

People have learned a lot by sending animals into space.
But it's very dangerous, and many of them haven't survived the trip.
That's why the use of laboratory animals has always been criticized.

25

People in space: the first steps

For ages, human beings have been dreaming of exploring the universe. But it's only been in the last sixty years that we've been able to make real steps forward.

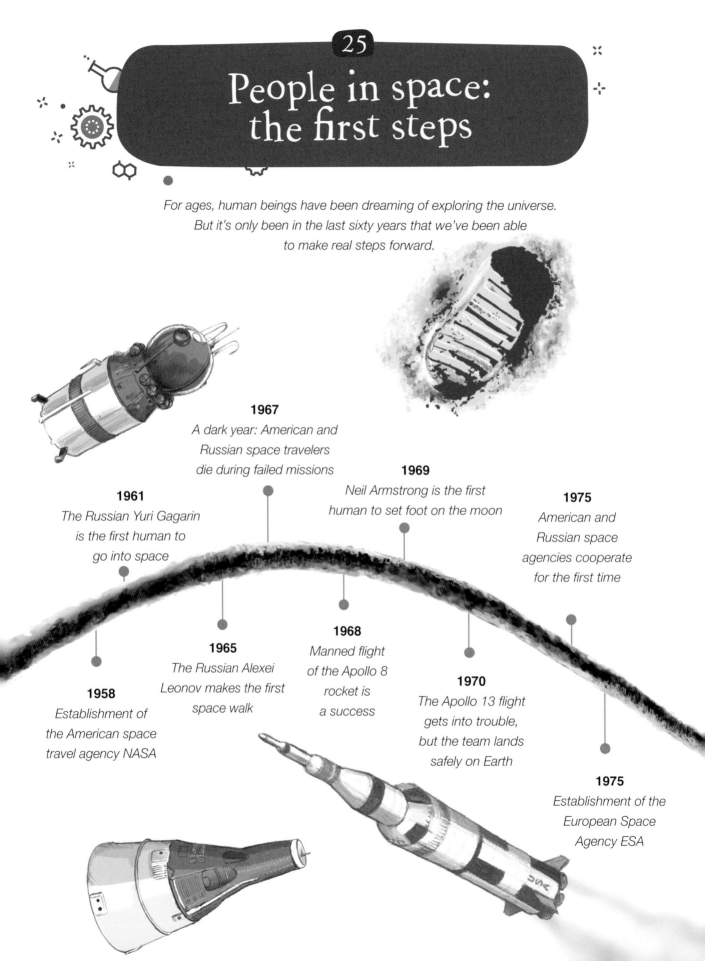

1967
A dark year: American and Russian space travelers die during failed missions

1969
Neil Armstrong is the first human to set foot on the moon

1975
American and Russian space agencies cooperate for the first time

1961
The Russian Yuri Gagarin is the first human to go into space

1958
Establishment of the American space travel agency NASA

1965
The Russian Alexei Leonov makes the first space walk

1968
Manned flight of the Apollo 8 rocket is a success

1970
The Apollo 13 flight gets into trouble, but the team lands safely on Earth

1975
Establishment of the European Space Agency ESA

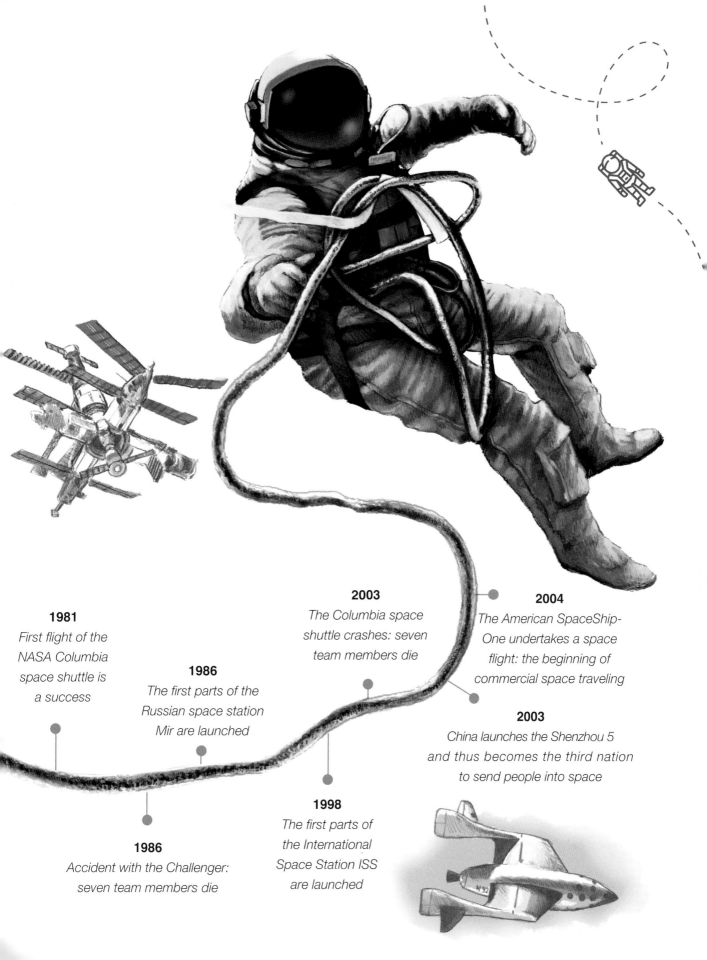

1981
First flight of the NASA Columbia space shuttle is a success

1986
The first parts of the Russian space station Mir are launched

2003
The Columbia space shuttle crashes: seven team members die

2004
The American SpaceShip-One undertakes a space flight: the beginning of commercial space traveling

2003
China launches the Shenzhou 5 and thus becomes the third nation to send people into space

1986
Accident with the Challenger: seven team members die

1998
The first parts of the International Space Station ISS are launched

26

Living in space

Luckily, astronauts don't have to constantly travel back and forth to outer space. Huge space stations have been built, where they can live for a while.

The first

Salyut 1 was the first space station. In 1971, the Russian construction was sent into orbit around the earth. Three cosmonauts lived there for twenty-three days.

Recycling

In 1973, the American Skylab was sent into orbit around the earth. To save money, existing rocket parts were reused. A large hydrogen tank from a Saturn V rocket was transformed into a living and working unit.

A fine

At the end of the mission, Skylab was meant to burn down in the atmosphere. But this plan didn't succeed entirely, and small parts of the space station crashed down in Australia. The space agency NASA was fined for this: 400 Australian dollars had to be paid for the illegal dumping of trash.

Mir

The Russian space station Mir consisted of various parts or modules: new modules were added on to one central module. From 1986 until 1999, Mir has been occupied almost continuously by various astronauts.

Stayer

The Russian space traveler Valeri Polyakov once stayed in space for 437 days. A world record!

A giant

The most famous and largest space station is the International Space Station ISS. The colossus is as large as a soccer field and about 65 feet (20 meters) high. The gigantic construction was built, manned, and paid for by various nations.

27

Living on Mars

The dream destination of a lot of space travelers? Mars! Will we ever visit this planet for real?

Set out for Mars

For decades, scientists have been working on plans for sending people to Mars. Primarily to do research, but also to start a colony and to live there!

DIY planet

One of the challenges for future inhabitants of Mars is that the planet is still completely deserted. There are no shops, houses, roads, food . . . Everything people need, they'll have to make themselves. That's why there's a lot of research going on about what materials there are on Mars and how they could be used.

That's profound research! This Mars lander looks deep into the ground of Mars.

Why not yet?

Mars is not an easy place to visit. It's very far away: a one-way ride takes about eight months. Besides, the planet is dusty and dry, without a habitable atmosphere. Humans need a space suit to survive. For the time being, we are focused on sending devices and robots to explore.

But later?

Yet, there are reasons why someone would like to go to Mars. We could do research there: Mars and Earth resemble each other, so perhaps we can learn a lot from Mars. Furthermore, it could be a fantastic adventure!

Then when will we go?

Nobody knows for certain when we will go to Mars. But some space agencies believe it will be before 2030. So, we just have to have a little patience . . . .

On Mars, you can find a rock called basalt. This rock could be a useful material.

28

DIY research

Of course, all those rockets, satellites, and Mars landers are fantastic. But even without those devices, you can observe a lot by yourself!

The sun
You cannot miss it! But never observe it without the right eye protection. Even a couple of seconds of bright sunlight might damage your sight.

The moon
Our most loyal friend. Sometimes, you can even see it at daytime!

Stars
See if you can find the astrological signs, such as the Big Dipper and the Small Dipper.

The Milky Way
Our little street in the universe. It's visible only when it's very clear and when there's no artificial lighting.

The planets
Some planets can be seen with the naked eye. They're like bright white spots in the sky.

The Orion Nebula
On clear winter evenings, you can see this cloud of dust, hydrogen, and gas.

The Andromeda Galaxy
That vague spot is a complete galaxy!

Satellites
If you watch carefully, you can see satellites orbiting the earth.

The ISS
Please wave at the International Space Station ISS. There are people inside!

Special phenomena
Can you detect meteor showers or eclipses of the moon and the sun?

All these things can be seen with the naked eye.

With help of binoculars or a telescope

Even with a rather simple telescope, you can see way further in the universe than with the naked eye. You could, for example, see the rings of Saturn or Jupiter with its four largest moons. And even closer, you can detect the frayed edges of the craters on the moon.

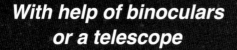

In an astronomical observatory

There are observatories where amateur astronomers look at the stars. Usually, you will find a large telescope through which visitors may have a look. Trained workers give explanations about what you can see. Often, there are other activities like lectures and movie performances.

How to become an astronomer

Are you fascinated by the universe? Do you want to contribute to the progress and knowledge of humankind? Would you like to unravel the riddles of the universe? Then perhaps being an astronomer is the right job for you!

It's not easy to become an astronomer. In the first place, you must love learning and do really well in school. You'll need good grades in physics and math. And you'll need to be determined and focused.

When you've graduated, it may not be easy to find a job as an astronomer. There aren't many positions. But don't let this stop you. In the end, there's always a demand for new professional astronomers, and maybe you'll be one of them!

Besides, if it won't be your profession, no problem! You can also choose to become an amateur astronomer, because even then you can make a lot of discoveries about the universe.

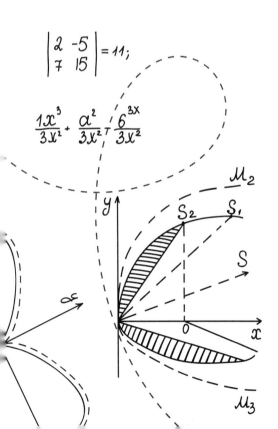

How to become an astronaut

Making a spacewalk, walking on the moon, or beginning a colony on Mars. There are a lot of people who dream about those things. But who may really go into space?

To be honest: there are only very few people who can have a career as an astronaut. The requirements are high, and only the very top of the qualified people will have the opportunity to become an astronaut.

SPACE EXPLORER

TO THE MOON

SPACE

OVER THE MOON

If you would be an astronomer

If you became an astronomer, what would your life be like? You probably think that you'll work at night, so you can look through a telescope. And yes, that's true, a lot of astronomers use telescopes. But why? What would they like to see? The rings of Saturn or the craters on the moon?

Astronomers hope to be able to solve riddles. Riddles like: how big is the universe, where does everything come from, and is there life somewhere else in space?

Those are only three of the many questions scientists ask themselves when they study the universe. We don't know the answers to those questions yet, but we do know something. That's because telescopes become more and more powerful, and astronomers work hard to learn as much as possible.

When your grandparents were as young as you're now, a lot of things you've read in this book weren't known yet. The moons of Jupiter, for example, could only be seen as tiny light spots. Now, with satellites, we've seen those moons from nearby. We can see clearly what the surface looks like, and we can even map it.

But we're not there yet. Numerous riddles still have to be solved by the astronomers of the future . . . and maybe by you!

Seth Shostak
Astronomer at the SETI Institute.

Many thanks to:
Arie Nouwen from Astroblogs, a real space fan who's read and checked
everything in this book, and **Seth Shostak** from the SETI Institute
for his bright insights and input.

Thanks for your help and expertise!